Pecking Order
Nicole Homer

CR

Write Bloody Publishing
America's Independent Press

Los Angeles, CA

1st edition.
ISBN: 978-1938912-72-6

Interior Layout by Cassidy Trier
Cover Designed by Dania Frink
Author Photo by Maria Del Naja
Proofread by Florence Davies
Edited by Jeanann Verlee
Type set in Bergamo from www.theleagueofmoveabletype.com

Printed in Tennessee, USA

Write Bloody Publishing
Los Angeles, CA
Support Independent Presses
writebloody.com

To contact the author, visit www.nicolehomer.com

MADE IN THE USA

Pecking Order

Nicole Homer

PECKING ORDER

The Overlap..13

Lottery..14

Lithopedians and Flesh...15

Conception...18

Portrait of My Grammama on Her Grammama's Lap,
     Neither of Them Smiling...21

Townies..22

Yes..23

How I Became a Mother Contemplating Loss.....................................24

Why Didn't You Just Go Look?...27

The Woman Who Is Not the Nanny Answers at the Grocery
     Store Concerning the, Evidently, Mismatched Children
     in and around Her Cart..28

But if You Are a *White Boy*, Then My Father Was a
White Boy, Too...31

I Have Counted Sixteen and a Half Dead Deer on
     My Ride Home from Work..32

The Paper Trail..34

Hunger...36

Ease...37

Things Only a Black Mother Can Prepare You For...............................38

The Grandmother Says [The Mother Thinks].....................................40

In Which I Use the DVR to Speak to
     the Paused Face of Michonne...41

The Mother Offers Advice (Or, I Am Doing the Best I Can
     with What I Have)...42

A Sister Remembers...45

The Colorist...48

Motherhood...52

I Count One Deer, Route 537..53
My Father Had Such Good Taste in Women......................54
Miss Celie...57
Things I Want to Say to Rae Dawn Chong.......................58
I Sit, Framed...60
The Women in the Family..61
Family Mythology...63
Casual Racist...66
Threshold..68
The Children Speak:..70
When I Had Children with a White Person.......................73
//if you say it is...75
I Wish I Was More Mothers..76

THE OVERLAP

Once a girl I love miscarried.
I didn't ask for details;
here is all I need to know:
she loved it
and it died.
I know, too, how the machine
works its sticky magic.
I have felt it unwork in me.
These are the details you need:
I didn't want it
and it died.
You need to know this, too:
I still think of it.
Want and love are not the same word.
When I was weeks into the making
of a wanted thing
there was a night
when she felt the stab of the machine
bucking
and I felt, instead, a kick.

LOTTERY

I went to every prenatal appointment. I went to a specialist because of my age. Because of the C-section two years ago. Because *the stress on the walls of the uterus.* Because *the scar.* Because no one trusts a woman's body. I put my feet in the stirrups. I took all the vitamins. I got enough sleep. I tried. I worked. But I had to work. I ate well. I don't even like avocados but they kept saying *good fat* so I ate. And I talked to him. I listened to his heartbeat. I told him I loved him. And when he kicked, I laughed even if I winced first. And when he pressed his hand against my organs like he wasn't going to stay there for another month or week, I didn't press back. I rubbed his palm through my body and felt him relax. And I relaxed. And they said I couldn't do a VBAC—no vaginal birth after cesarean for us, they said—but we knew better, him and me. We knew we could. And when it started to trickle out of me like the slow start of an ugly cry, I wasn't scared. I pushed when they asked me to push. I breathed when they asked me to breathe. I screamed without asking anyone's blessing. They handed him to me and he was at once and still my love. But. But he was as pale as the ghost of a black boy.

Lithopedians and Flesh

A lithopedian is a stone baby; dead inside its mother, it calcifies.
It was 1948.
Her name is not important
The war had been over for three years.
This is what the history books will tell you,
as though peace is a sudden thing:
a light switch
or a veil dropped over a country.
The newspapers will not mention her—
nothing about this thirty-two-year old woman
or the kicking she harbored inside her.
How it was a soft
insistent tapping at first,
its own war drum,
how her hand circled
her belly like a battleship
or bird of prey
a hand—a woman's hand—casting a spell.
No, they will only announce: *PEACE!*
as though quiet is something every woman would want.
The tapping was insistent
until it wasn't.
When the doctors used the word *dead*,
she did not become someone else;
she remained what she was:
poor, survivor, woman.
When they said *operation* and *expensive*,
her hand circled the new graveyard
like a vulture.

Leave it be, she said.
And they did.

———

Because it's easy and simple,
I want to believe
nature offers just two options:
rot or harden.

———

It is 1994.
The tree in my backyard is full of plums.
Some of them:
hard green stones.
Some of them:
sweet and black and burst,
split open on the lawn.
Any old woman will tell you:
to ripen a thing,
put it in the dark;
a bag will do
or a cupboard with a door that closes.
They will also tell you
the sweetest plum is the one on the verge of rot.

———

I was 16.
I knew some things grew in the dark;
I did not know I was made of dark.
I was 16:
sweet and black and burst.
The old women did not tell me that we ripen hard,

that the body can close like a small green fist
around anything it deems rotten,
that this is how pearls and memories and women are made:
in the 17th gestational week,
the hardening:
the soft, growing cartilage architecture
slowly starts to become bone.
The old women never told me when it will stop.
The old men say that only the strong survive
but, I am a woman, I know Goliath dies,
and I imagine some small, frail woman
was paid to wash his massive body before his funeral.
It is the resourceful, the determined
who live long enough to nurse their young.
I am not 16 anymore
I am not sweet to bursting anymore—
but how that year still walks my hallways,
how it curls up inside me
like a smooth and sunken stone.

CONCEPTION

I'm already twenty minutes late when I walk out into the street.
It's cold and raining and I know from the café's mirrored windows
and the pride of dogs humming in unison
that I am inside a song my mother is singing.
That is no sun but her voice,
rising, rising, rising.
Song is another thing I will not get from her.
I wonder if I am in her throat or her lungs.
It doesn't look how I thought it would;
though she has never been there I think my mother is made of Paris.
I wish she were made of blood
of changing viscosity
of photographs, even.
I wish she was familiar.
There is a newspaper blowing down the main street—the rue.
Wind pins it to my shoe.
I try to pick it up but it is heavy as a corroded anchor.
I can read the headlines: three birth announcements.
It *is* an anchor now,
shaped like Cerberus, and hungrier.
The clouds are a thousand milkless nipples.
I think: if I could get to her mouth
I could crawl out of her
like a high note,
light and scarless.
I can feel her breathing,
the windows swell and deflate.
Everything is alive here. I wish I had worn more sensible shoes,
combed my hair or, at least, looked in the mirror

before I left.
I wonder if I have on clean underwear,
if I have eaten,
if she will have me.
I realize I am the only person on the sidewalk, a pack of dogs behind me.
The windows are still convexing and concaving
and every other face in Paris is inside them:
the bookstores, the coffee shops, the tailor's front room.
I want desperately for the tailor to make me a dress.
I press my nose to the glass and watch him:
he uses his picketfence teeth to hem the dress.
The model is twenty and her breasts point up at the ceiling like tourists.
She doesn't seem to mind the bite;
in the mouth of the store
the pinch of each incisor
makes the dress fit like a new name.
When she sees me, she reapplies her makeup—
more rouge this time.
She is not blushing. She is singing.
Behind me, a semi-circle of un-collared and wagging tails
hum along with her.
She pulls a baton from her purse;
we, a chorus of strays, howl.
It sounds as though we have never been full.
When the song is over, she pierces the window with a flash of her smile.
Every dog rushes in to tear at her dress;
we have never been hungrier.
Her lungs are a delicacy,
therefore, the last thing I eat.

She tastes just like Paris
which is odd:
I know she'll never get there with so many bloodhounds
eating her.

Portrait of My Grammama on Her Grammama's Lap, Neither of Them Smiling

They say I got her nose,
not sure I see it. Sometimes I want to
go back to being small
enough to fit on her lap.
You might think I'm unhappy
here, but this a picture 'bout joy.
What you know 'bout me and my grammama
on that bench? What song I could sing
make you understand? It takes so long
to force a moment into a photograph. She held me
in place. Her hands strong 'round me
where would grow my hips.
Them I got from her. And her sly smile
what creeps across our face like a thief.
Us two sitting there
like stillness a luxury we was used to.

TOWNIES

No one lives in The Town of Motherhood,
but me
says every mother
including me.
I did not see another woman's body
in the room
at midnight,
when the children were dislodged from me like
splinters.
I did not see another woman's body
as one hungry mouth
after another
took from me sleep and vitamins, uncompromising.
There was no voice in my ear,
no common incantation
that might unchafe
or uncrack me,
unbloody my nipple.
All these children
came from someone,
including me.
When the left shoe is inexplicably missing
when crumbs gather like a choir to sing my inadequacies
from the deep of a two-day-old bra
at midnight,
at naptime
no one lives here
but me.

YES

it's a body   it's not your body   but isn't it   isn't that your mother
her hair   your grandmother's wrist   itsnotmeitsnotmeitsnotme   you repeat
you touch your body   your fingers   digging into the give of flesh
and the resist of bone   to assure yourself that it still *is*   you
pick pick pick at your cuticle   summon your blood to the surface
to prove that it has not congealed   and that it still *is*   isn't it
your body awake and moving   and looking so much like   that body
which is neither   your mother's or your grandmother's or   yours
and you have to name it: the death that keeps   knocking
you think if you say the words into the air   you can conjure   the body
but when you open your mouth all that rushes out   is your name
is that which you will someday share with death but not this death and then
you notice her mouth   how it once was teeth and curve of lips
and you stop smiling   wanting nothing at all to do   with joy
but now you look even more like the body   even less like you
still here in this room in your notyettaken skin and that's the trick, isn't it?

How I Became a Mother Contemplating Loss

A wall of fliers stare at me as I wait to buy postage. In my arms, a box full of clothes my children have lived in and outgrown. Seven states away my oldest friend has a daughter small enough to need these things. In fifth grade, the two of us lit fires on the asphalt of an overgrown tennis court; now we mail clothes.

The children pinned to the wall are dated then re-imagined older. Only two boxes: *then* and *now, maybe.* This is the scariest thing: a mother without even a body to mourn. Not ash or DNA evidence. Not even a failure of justice. I cannot smell my children through the box in my arms and I am angry that I washed the clothes before bringing them here. A selfish parent, I would not part even with their scents.

I was born dreaming I would die in childbirth. Always the same thick, red dream. A screeching and wailing woman on the table. I am cold and there are faces—so many faces—all around me, but I am alone. There are voices. They do not talk to me. Then, I am gone and the only echo I leave is this new gasp for air, this new cry.

When I found out I was pregnant, I nested in the dark, imagining myself octopus or goddess. I cleaned my house and labeled the important papers so my love would know where things were when he and the babies came home from the hospital without me.

I did not die. I let a stranger razor me open in a white room. That was the worst smell: bleach and copper, clean metal and my own exposed insides. The worst sound: my love's fearful breath twelve inches from my tears. Then: the surgeon asking the nurse *Why is she crying?* I, tied to the table, plastic-Jesus stretched out, wanted her to kill her, then. I want to kill her now. The woman with the razor: lice-mouthed rat, feather-less crow, rabid and balding cat.

And this is the beast who brought me my daughters. This is the merchant who sent me home to the labels my love did not need. This is woman who keeps my death in a box on a shelf in her office. It sits there with all the other deaths staring out at her degrees and starched white coats, hooked by the collar and hanging.

It is not a comfort to not have died on that table. To be given, not one but two small mouths. So I went to meet my blood again, to hear it sing a second time. To pray with my only body every prayer I swallowed as a child: Dear [ ] let me live longer than my father. Dear [ ] let me go. Dear [ ] let them love me. Dear [ ] let me forget this. Dear [ ] let some-one answer.

Pregnant again, I answered. I, alive and fortress and brick tenement and splintered treehouse, answered my want. My body offered me a new dream: a woman as round as I, reaching into me; a room, dimly lit and gray; voices talking to me; tears and sweat and shit and blood, my blood, my screams. Then, my newest prayer on my chest. Hungry for my body and suckling at me until we were both milk drunk and near sleep. My milk in his mouth the sweetest thing I have ever lived through.

I held him for hours that way. His hair flaked with my blood. His skin sticky with my blood. His blood, my blood.

In the end there were five of us: me, knife and whetstone; my love, sheath and hacksaw; the youngest, mallet and wheel; my middle child, crowbar and mirror; the oldest by a minute: serrated blade and sand-paper. I don't have the dream anymore. I peeled each label off. My love will have to figure it out when my death finally crawls out of that box and comes to sing me home.

That is the scariest thing:

that we do it anyway. The blood, the screams, the milk.

That seven states away there is a woman who understands. Who chose, as I did, to risk the razor a first—a second time. That in this post office, there are women whose guts smile from the blade. That in the states between us, there are too many to count. That my mother told me it was the most painful thing she ever experienced in her life. And I am the youngest of three. That for each of these fliers someone razored a woman a second time and there was no cry, no limp body, no blood.

I touch my scar through my jeans and imagine a silence as bright white as an operating room and a body, small made entirely of sympathy cards and *missing* fliers—in my arms—
then gone.

Why Didn't You Just Go Look?

I had not slept for months
when the baby first quieted through the night.
It sat in the bed with me: the still air.
Hunched over, its elbows on its knees,
head in its hands.
We waited like that, like two women
in the stark pastel of a hospital,
for the answer to the alwaysquestion:
is my child [expectant look
where I dare not place the adjective]?

THE WOMAN WHO IS NOT THE NANNY ANSWERS AT THE GROCERY STORE CONCERNING THE, EVIDENTLY, MISMATCHED CHILDREN IN AND AROUND HER CART

I stabbed her,
the skinny-half-caff in the high-waisted yoga pants
so I can only assume that she is still in the alley
behind this fine establishment
bleeding out. I aimed for the femoral artery.
Hopefully it was quick and painless—
as painless as these things can be.
What I like to do,
after a kill,
is abduct the children of my victim
and then—this is my unique signature
my M.O. if you will—
I like to take the children on mundane errands.
That's why we're here: buying
frozen, microwavable chicken nuggets
because nothing quite says *murderous spree*
like organic chicken breasts
dipped in a seven whole grain bread mixture.

I couldn't help but notice how hungry your children look.
No, no. Don't stop now.
I'm enjoying the very specific
and prying questions that you
are levying at me.
There's a level of brutal honesty
that I can only achieve with
a complete stranger:
for instance, this one—my boy,

it was so hard to get him.
I had to practically bribe the IVF doctor
to put that white woman's eggs in me.
It feels good to say that out loud.
These two? They aren't even twins.
I stole one from a yoga instructor
busy berating the barista at Whole Foods.

This does feel good.
Let's pick up some hummus
then head to aisle 3 for chips.
I have so many questions for you:
about your home training
about the one in your cart and his uncleft chin.

I don't know what you'd call me
in relation to them. I:
feed them; dress them; read them stories.
And I have been called things so much worse than nanny;
you know that, though, don't you?
They're adopted. All of them. These. The three brats
in aisle 9. The unattended one in Dairy. The two screaming
for a mother in checkout. All of them.
I've been eyeing yours.
I'm starting a band. We're going to do only cover songs.
Only Sly and the Family Stone. Or only Ted Nugent.
I'm still deciding. I know we can only be one thing
or the other.

Do you need a nanny? Can that one in the cart hit a high E?
Are you in the market for childcare services? How are her teeth?
I'm truly sorry that I don't have a resume
or list of references handy.
The nanny position
that you have made up during this brief conversation sounds
delightful. Especially the detail about traveling with the family.
I, too, like to have the help with me.
I mean can I really be trusted to care for these
mixed-matched children here
on my own?
Do you know hard it is to get the blood of strangers
out of cotton?

Oh, look at your girl smiling up at me; I think she likes me.

BUT IF YOU ARE A *WHITE BOY*, THEN MY FATHER WAS A *WHITE BOY*, TOO.

The only thing I ever did worthy of the word *traitor*:
love you but call you *white boy*
when you weren't around.
As if I selected you from a shelf
where all the white boys sat:
light haired, light eyed, thin lipped. Interchangeable.
I am sorry. I did it more than once.
I am sorry. I meant it every time.

I Have Counted Sixteen and a Half Dead Deer on My Ride Home from Work

My mother, who lives unmistakably in the suburbs, calls to tell me there are deer in her backyard, that they sprinted across the street, through the neighbors' poorly manicured lawn, and out of sight. *It's deer mating season,* she tells me. I should be careful.

My mother is full of useful facts tonight. *If you can't avoid hitting the deer,* she says, *if it becomes inevitable, brake as much as you can right up until you are about to hit it. Then let go of the brake.* If I do this, my car will run over the deer instead of the deer going over the hood, which we both know means through the windshield.

My mother watches the news too much and is always trying to save me. *They're in heat; I don't think they even see the road or the cars or anything. They'll kill you, y'know? And themselves, too.* I don't ask where she heard the tidbit about the braking. I don't tell her that I doubt I'll remember it in a crisis.

My mother, who has been burying my father for twenty-one years, does not trust me. I am alive and that could change at any moment. Forgetting her advice would be unforgivable. She does not trust the deer, either. Or the brakes. Or arteries. Or police officers. Or seats belts. Or EMT workers. *You never know,* she says. I do not tell her I am on my cell phone, that she is my accomplice in this clearly distracting and il-legal activity.

My mother has been talking to me for five minutes about something dangerous and how to avoid it. I cannot hear her; I, having made the turn into my driveway, am composed entirely of my sense of sight: my husband's car sits staring at me.

I am off the phone. I am in the house. I don't remember how I got here; I imagine I walked up the long driveway and opened the backdoor. I am smiling at him. I am hugging him. I am smelling him. I do not trust myself. I do not trust him. I do not know how to brake. I am afraid of my mother's shovel: when the time comes, I will bury him for as long as it takes.

The Paper Trail

In the driveway, the soft squeaking toys and jagged gravel press into
each other. In the kitchen, the dishes, dirty and chipped, are piled in
the sink. The dining room the table is almost imaginary, under the
crayons, pencils, papers. In the hallway, the family stares out from
twenty-three neatly framed pictures. In the bathroom, the shower is
dirty; the floor wet. In the bedroom, hoses connect each of her breasts
to the mouths of the hungry pump. This is domestic commerce: she
trades her fatty milk for the white noise of the pump. Everything is an
exchange: one thing for another. Once, she was a woman. Once, her
cheeks were dry in the afternoons; now, wet always. Emptied, she turns
the machine off, washes the durable plastic in the sink, stares at the
childless neighbors' house, into an uncluttered living room and pictures
herself alone. No dust, no laundry, no sticky surfaces, no refrigera-
tor scabbed with construction paper. It would be a clean life. A lawyer
could bleach it all with just signed papers. Instead, she washes her hand
with a quick pump of dollar store soap. Her heart looks nothing like
the hand-drawn pictures pinned under magnets. It is not a wanderer.
She has chosen other adventures: nurse the baby; find a new fixture
for the sink; figure out why the floor around the washer is always just
a little wet; get a spare key to the front door cut; ask the GYN: *Why
can't I get wet?* There is so much to do. She's learning origami. Folding
and refolding paper into swans. She sets them free in the sink, hurries
her breast to the unforgiving mouths: the baby, the pump. Looking
down at it, she compares this one to the others. They all look cuter in
pictures. This is not what she pictured. In the hallway, a photograph:
her, before. Before the two wet stains on every shirt. Before the the first
babies. Before the other one. Before the table was buried under enve-
lopes and unwanted papers. Before the most reliable mouth at her nip-
ple was a pump. That was before; now is a ship that will not sink. Swans

34

and stars and cranes sail into yesterday's macaroni and cheese, still floating in the sink. So many open mouths surround her. She can't picture silence. This tornado is its own kind of peace, constructed from broken fuel pumps and dry macaroni crushed underfoot and all this flesh—dirty and wet. The cranes could unfold themselves, give up their delicate bodies, and become, once more, paper. Then she could not tell one creased corpse from the other. The water creeps up through their bodies and they sink. Everything is one thing then another. She realizes how paper thin her skin will be at ninety. Eventually her own child will leave her breast empty and aching for its wet. One day, her hand on the gas pump, she will remember how flammable she was.

HUNGER

When I speak of hunger, I speak of the new mouth. Praise the tooth-less appetite that is instinct alone. I point to my bloodied nipple. I speak of the wince my body remembers. I speak of a small mouth wrapped around the pain of me learning what to do. Praise the blood-tinged milk. I have never known a hunger as unembarrassed as the opened mouth of a four-pound baby. Praise the engorged breasts that woke me in the night before the crying did. I speak of my body, hungry for the toothless mouth's hunger. Praise the nipple that heals slowly, but heals. Praise the milk. Praise, even, the stained shirts. I speak of evidence that the thought of a hungry mouth has made me consumable. When I speak of hunger, I speak of our bodies and become a mouth.

EASE

What is motherhood but a wanting:
the child to have more better easier.
But I did not want this for him:
to look like an easy life
while we look like we do
like kin like bodies in a newsfeed like hard.
How can I wish hardship upon him?
Where we do not overlap, how will we touch?

What can I teach him about a world
that will let him move through it
as if he owns it? My rage
will be a foreign thing. A gift I might try to give him
not knowing what I expect him to do with it,
in what pocket he might carry it.
With him, this repeated betrayal
of skin. Every day we will continue to look like kin
who aint kin. To the son I made with my black body:
what has a blue-eyed boy ever done
with a black woman's anger
but cause it?

Things Only a Black Mother
Can Prepare You For

The oldest sat in the passenger seat. He grew his first mustache
at thirteen. His little brother's chest was still a birdcage
sitting in the backseat of his best friend's Chevy. Jason was
crooked gap grin, dirty jokes, and the only white face. Among the five boys,
he was the smallest by one and a quarter inches. His dick jokes
all had the same punch line. Jason sat in the backseat
between two black boys, each of them next to a rolled down window.
In the front, two more black boys, two more open windows.
All five sang in unison with the radio and prayed
to the same god. For years now they had whispered
in the back of their church
about girls who stood in the front of the church whispering
about them. The four black boys in the car
thought about their mothers when they passed the sedan,
white and unmarked. Jason sat in the middle of the backseat
with no warning rising up in him. His mother had never bought flowers
for a young man's funeral or advised her son
how to avoid attending his own:
Say *Yes, Officer* and *No, Officer. Keep your hands on the wheel.*
Every boy but Jason breathed deep and remembered their lines.
When the red and blue noise tangled in the air above the car,
the Chevy answered by bringing its body,
already more rusted than when they left home,
to the shoulder of the road. Four of the boys
were pale as dead men. The officer pulled them all out of the car
with only his voice and badge. Jason was praying to the same god
his friends were. Those four black boys, eyeing the blue uniform
and the same face it always wore. Jason got half-hidden sideways looks

when the officer pulled him away from the others
and spoke to him in hushed tones: Are you okay?
He did not understand. In the side view mirror, he saw his friends.
The man's eyes repeated, Are you okay? He stepped closer
to the boy, close enough to offer the secret handshake
of his concern: With them? Jason's friends, several feet and a world away,
stood staring at the ground, looking apologetic, thinking
of their mothers, of black dresses, of their own crime scene faces.
Jason, somehow whiter now than when they had left home, nodded
like an apology to the boys he grew up with. Back in the car,
the radio offered up a song they could all sing like a hymn to the same god.

THE GRANDMOTHER SAYS [THE MOTHER THINKS]

These people better be glad I found Jesus
[This is how I know my mother
thought about hitting the woman in the store.]
how she gonna almost break her neck looking at us
then tryin' act like she aint just do a double, a triple take
[I don't know what to do with my hands—Jesus has always eluded me—
I fold my arms, lean against her kitchen wall, look out the window.
Maybe he's in the neighbor's yard.]
It's so funny to see their faces. I know you know,
but they half fall and hurt themselves trying to figure out
who this little [she is careful not to say white] boy is to me
then when he screams out *grandma* I have to try
so hard not to laugh at their eyes
buggin' out of their faces. [she doubles over, now,
under the weight of the repeated scene, its hilarity.]
You know I know how to act and talk
[She dusts off the voice we use to open doors]
so I just go about my business in the store
like I don't see them.
And I say stuff like, [She adjusts her posture. Now, each vertebra
and syllable are aligned, distinct but cooperating.]
now what are we going to have for lunch today?
[She returns to herself, to me.]
Proper because you know I know how to talk and they expectin'
well I don't know what they expectin', but
it aint me.

In Which I Use the DVR to Speak to the Paused Face of Michonne

Everyone expects you
to be my favorite. *You must be angry*
they say to me. At meetings,
I do not smile
but I aint mad at you. About your face,
I often wonder which episode it was
that first contorted your mouth into something
resembling pleasant. I can smile, too.
I did not want to like you. Because we are alike:
you are angry and black and woman—
a predictable favorite for me to have.
And you are. You, second-hand katana. You,
home-taught death. You have my mother's
hands: slender fingers wringing and wringing
til not a drop of water remains in the clothes.
She is like us: angry and black and woman
and I don't want to know what her hands have done
in the service of our family. I don't want to tell the truth
about what I have done. You can keep a secret.
I wanted to be something else. But still like her,
I snap at the white women in the mall who stare,
say *hello* too loudly for it to be friendly. You
let a lover follow you around for how many years?
His mouth ajar, empty. You are not friendly either.
And what are we but evidence
in the case made against us?
Lean in close so I can tell you the truth:
I have never wanted to be anything else.
Except, perhaps, you.

The Mother Offers Advice (Or, I Am Doing the Best I Can with What I Have)

1859

To my girls who are light but would not have passed:

Smile. Don't sass. Don't do nothing get no extra attention. You don't want no extra attention from nobody 'round here. You get some, don't go thinking it's a blessing. Watch out for the Missus. For Massa's fickleness. He don't never like one thing for too long. That's how he is with Missus. Why they marry but aint no one 'round here get no relief for long. That's why you aint seen Margret round here since before he got that wife. Sold. And for what? So he could play at marrying. It aint gonna be long 'fore he back to playin' at adulterin'. Don't let it be you. But if it you: be whatever he want. Just don't be sold. You know what it means to be yellow and a girl and halfway decent looking? Means some of your children might get out of this alive. If they boys.

To my son who could pass:

Run.

Be poor and white. Be some white orphan boy. Run. Forget us. Forget me. Forget you were ever black. Run so far away that the stench of "owned" aint on you no more. Run farther than dogs can follow. Lie and lie and lie about who you are and build a life on that lie. If you get money, buy your sisters. Or at least their children. They'll be like you I figure with the way Massa look at those girls of mine. I know that look. Run. Don't never tell nobody who your mama is.

1963

To my daughters:

Don't come home full of some white boy's joyride. Don't be a field trip to the colored side of town. Flattery is quick and cheap and won't feed nobody. But your body aint an apology owed to black men either. Just 'cause you got it easier than they do. And you do: got it easier some ways. Still have to fight same as the men. But know that when they come for the men's flesh, they will leave it ash and lesson. But if they get to you: they will leave it lesson, but full of breath. And maybe more. You aint some white gal. Don't you never let me hear you needed to be reminded of that.

To my Son:

Sit at the counter and be called what you are not: race traitor. They will think you a weak white boy, call you nigger lover. And I smile, 'cause you are. 'Cause you mine and you love me and you love us and you love you. And you black. You aint no race traitor, but you better use that body in this fight. If I'm using mine.

Go where we can't. Every *whites only* hotel bar. Every unmolested voting booth. Every neighborhood outlined in red.

Hear what we can't. Every joke. Every underbreath slur. Every sheriff's laugh that aint meant for us. You catch them in your pale hand. Leave this color you got—that I gave you - in you everything you touch. This is what you are: a weapon only a mother could love.

2017

Daughters:

Don't let that hair have you thinking you're cute or you aint black as me. You lighter than me. I'm lighter than grandma. And we all still black. We black women. All of us. Know that aint nobody coming to rescue you but us. No White Feminist got time for this. No black liberation revolution got you on its posters. You know how many black women died the summer Mike Brown did? Me neither because nobody gave a fuck. Get a degree but don't think it'll save you. Get a husband or wife or kids or a house, but don't think you aint this. Everywhere. All the time.

You need saving, you call me. I'll come. Pick up grandma on the way.
Like we always done.

Son:

I'm your mother. How you aint gonna be black? Look at me. Look at
your grandma. I don't care whose blue eyes you got, I made you with
my body. My black black body. First body you ever touched was black.
Don't let nobody tell you different. Don't let nobody patrol these bor-
ders around blackness like you aint allowed in. I paid your way.

But, you gotta pay, too.

A Sister Remembers

I was little too.
And I wouldn't remember
except. Mama's face.
The *dare you* face she saved
mostly for us.
But I saw her give it to that woman.
Once I spilled all my juice:
the table the floor my new pants.
Mama said, *Accidents happen.*
Let's try again.
Everything was clean after that.
Until my sister spilled her juice:
the table the floor the chair
I said *Mama! Mama! She spilled!*
You gon' get in trouble.
Mama, big and close, said *You know you*
just spilled more than this two minutes ago.
And you tryna make your sister feel bad?
Keep it up. I dare you.
Something about her face
was like she wasn't my mama when she said that
It was her mouth her nose her everything
but not.
Like at bedtime when she kissed us and said goodnight
and then darkness
everything was still there
but I couldn't see it.

We were on a bus
or a train—

lots of people who weren't us sitting close.
She was holding baby boy
She called us all that: baby boy or baby girl
He was sleep on her, his fat legs and wild blond hair
taking up too much space.
I wanted to be on her lap, too.
I was next to her instead. Her arm around my neck,
her finger sometimes playing in my brown curls.
All of us were sandy
between our toes and in our hair.
I remember the beach.
The water.
Me and mama out a little too far
holding hands,
us a circle.
Don't let go. I said it over and over.
Never, baby girl. Never.
There were two kids in seats across from us:
a boy and a girl
and their mom.
They were mostly speaking words I didn't understand
Then the woman said *Are they all yours?*
We had a lot of bags
a lot of towels that we had spread on the beach
and pretended to sleep on.
Dad said he was *tanning.* He was red now and standing almost next to us.
Mama said she wasn't never mad at getting darker
and laid like a starfish on the towel.
You'll get darker too, baby girl. Sun lotion won't stop it. And smiled.

All these towels were ours, but
Mama said *twins*
but we had more than two towels
and they weren't the same.
I am a twin. My sister, the other
baby girl, was on Mama's other side
close to the window.
Mama looked like the dark furniture in our room
that I can't see
that I thought was there
The woman, *Oh twins.*
Then, said it in French to her daughter,
who our sister, the friendliest of us all, had been smiling at.
You're so strong, she said
I'm tired from just two.
And like that, the light in Mama's face came back on.
But I wondered about it
not about the face she showed us
at the beach, in the restaurant, buying gelati
smiling and laughing and all the time
but the other one always in the dark
daring someone to say
something.

The Colorist

Oprah said it (or maybe I read it on a pillow or an Etsy totebag) so I believe it: The universe will give you opportunity after opportunity to learn a lesson. Endless opportunities until you get it. If you think you got it and the opportunity presents itself again, well...

Kiti yellower than me. We 11. The boys love her. Not just because she does not think she is one of them. She has a thick rope of hair hanging down past where her ass will be in two years. *You be out in the sun too much*, she says right after I do not say how cute I think David is. He has been circling her, his brother, too. And each of their best friends. Someone is going to get bloodied. This is what Kiti is worth.

When Kiti becomes the ornament on David's car in high school, I am invited to double-date his brother. I am still 11: makeupless, in my brothers' handmedowns, but yellow. I do not mind. It is so good to be wanted in the back seat of a car, to finally be someone's bad decision.

Lisa is all ass and waist. Perfect self-composed senior. She not yellow, not brown. They call her purpleblack at school. And I cannot help but think of plums when I see her. I wonder why isn't everyone else's mouth watering, too?

I am on the phone when he says *You must be talking to Lisa. I can smell the black.* I am stunned silent. I *am* talking to Lisa. Lisa *black*. But so is my mama and what? I am so quiet. I am so much blink and recoil. But I don't know from what. I don't even like Lisa that much. That's not true. I do. But I love my mother. That is true. But how did he know? But I was so quiet.

You're pretty for a black girl is a thing white boys say to me when they aren't bold enough to hit on the darker skinned girls they really want in high school. In college. At my first job. Yesterday. I'm not bold either, I guess. And I bring home a parade of beige. They are mostly good boys. But there is already a thumb on that scale in their favor.

You're pretty, redbone, is what the brown boys say when they are trying to fuck me. Not as pretty as my mama, I know. Not as pretty as Lisa, I know that, too. But who doesn't want to be called pretty? What plain girl can't ignore more than she should just to hear it?

I don't wear makeup. I feel like it means I am going to war. My mother has always worn makeup. My aunt has always worn makeup. Lisa has always worn makeup. How could I not know they've been at war this whole time? Lisa is in that war, too. And I'm not sure which side I'm on. There is a thumb on that scale, too. My mother is prettier than I can ever hope to be. I have seen her body in a bathtub so this is not humility. She not is pretty for a dark girl. But she is that, too. She is asterisk and caveat.

As a child at the store, people would stop to say what a pretty girl I was and I believed them. How could I know they meant *she does not look like you*? How could I know this was the real compliment? Why did she accept it? When she smiled a thank you at the old black women and the young WASPs, why were we both so happy? How could I not know we've been at war this whole time? What kind of soldier does that make me?

Before the kids, my love told me his dream: a boy with his face smiling and running someplace outside and idyllic. Maybe he and his dream son are doing some classic white people shit: crocheting, colonizing, whatever. He is so happy when he tells me he has had the dream for years. It repeats. It repeats. He says.

I say: *but you know it could be a girl, right?* This is not what I want to say, but I think it is a good lead in. *Yeah, I know* he says. And I believe he does.

You know that I'm black right? Yeah, he says. And he does. *So our kid wouldn't be white. You know that, right?* And he doesn't. Not in those terms. And I think: here is the lesson. Look at me, universe, helping him learn.

And when his son was finally born, looking just just like him, I thought: *Okay universe, you are a funny motherfucker. What am I supposed to be learning here?*

What the people in the store mean when they see me holding my son and ask me if I am the help is this: *He doesn't look like you.* And I don't know if this is a compliment. Or to whom. Is he cute for a black baby? But, no, I'm the only one who thinks of him like that. Is the woman in the cereal aisle congratulating me on erasing my mother from her own bloodline?

No one asks me if I am my daughters' mother. They Kiti yellow which, next to me, must seem at least possible which I know means preferable.

We were talking about school. About race. About diversity in the school system and he says *Well they don't look black so it'll be easier on them.* And I hated my love's body then. Which is not fair. But we did this to them: paled them. And this man wants me to congratulate myself. To thank my traitor womb.

All the dolls in my house are black. Not white. Not yellow. They are perfect skin and brown eyes. I buy the babies I thought I would have and give them to my children. I don't ask which dolls they want; I don't care. I am afraid of what they might choose. I won't bring any more white babies here willingly.

I never have.

MOTHERHOOD

Motherhood is like

                being pecked

      to death

                      by my

    favorite birds

                      made from my

                      body, torn

      by beaks sharpened

                      on the woman

          I was

                      when I slept more

          or sang the song I stole

          out of

          my mother's mouth

I Count One Deer, Route 537

slick
full of bloat
the neck's whimsical angle
an audience of plodding birds
their beaks
the cars slow down
much too late
to marvel at your body

My Father Had Such Good Taste in Women

In 1983, it was still possible to retire from a company you started working at right out of high school. Or trade school. Or after your day job as a gardener sun poisoned your back for the third time. Even though 1977 was not full of words like *melanoma* or *squamous cell* or *carcinoma,* your not-so-new wife was full of words like *caution* and *pale* and *future.* You gave up your motorcycle and your job outdoors where you had to eat in your old rusted red truck or in the garage because you were dirty and sweaty and so red and peeling and that might get on the carpet. But. You could use the bathroom; that was made clear by "lady of the house"—that's what your boss called her even when she wasn't there— because last year one of "your kind"—that's what she said to him, but not what he said to you—urinated in the bushes "like an animal."
In 1974, you thought that your kind was poor. Your wife was sure that "poor" in that white lady's mouth meant poor *and* Mexican *and* illegal, your wife she knew so much more than you about being brown and "the help" so even if you didn't believe her, you didn't contradict her. In 1975, "the lady of the house" sprung for good old American poor. Lucky you.
1976 was a good year to start night school, to learn about computing. Your wife had a big vocabulary and knew words like *caution* and *pale* and *future.* 1977 was a good year to quit your day job, go to school full time but it was a bad year to be married to you, an ex-gardener; it meant your wife on her knees bleaching the grout during the day and up with the oldest boy at night.
1977 was an okay year to be your second born; while your oldest wheezed, there were good toys in every waiting room to distract the newest mouth in the family. And soon, your family started to need things like antibiotics and orthodontia and a neighborhood where it was possible to come home from church and not find three men in your liv-

ing room and the contents of your home spread out in the alley—which you called a backyard—waiting to be loaded into a van. So you got a job at a company that still gave out gold watches and you showed up early every day for a year.

You computed. You cubicled and brown-bagged. You got a raise and a mortgage and a Nova that barely went. Your wife stopped bleaching things and your son started breathing. She cut your hair in a chair in the kitchen. She laid out ties and suits and matching handkerchiefs because you had bad taste in everything except women.

In 1983, you and your spouse, of course, got invited to dinner by your boss but, by then, you had three small children at home and politely declined because your wife told you that you were busy. And you were. At your desk, in your office, you were almost important now and better at computing than almost anyone in your company. You were not looking at pictures of your children when your boss walked in because your wife had forgotten, again, to leave out the framed school portraits. You did not have your family on display like all the other men on your floor. They didn't have children like yours. Or wives like yours, humming *caution* and *pale* and *future*.

Then your boss invited you in the way that an invitation is not an invitation to the company's annual dinner. And you said of course because of course. And of course you would bring your wife. And three weeks later she laid out your tie and suit and shoes and even socks because this was important. And you asked her to wear her navy blue dress and she said yes and you were surprised because you had bad taste in everything except women and you both knew it.

And at 6 o'clock she was in the bathroom, "not feeling well." So you went without her because you couldn't miss the gold watch extravaganza even if you barely knew the old man whose office would be empty next week. You went alone, in your tie and matching socks. When you got home, in 1985, your wife seemed curiously well. When you told her about the intricacies of cold cuts and corporate buffets, she smiled. When you reminded her that she had forgotten, again, to give you pictures of the kids for your desk she assured you that she would leave them out for you in the morning. She would not. She was so busy framing those words, *caution* and *pale* and *future*, and you never noticed anything except what good taste you had in women.

MISS CELIE

Miss Celie is snatched out of a family photo
when I see her on the screen. It is not her face exactly
that points to my grandmother. The man who Mistered her
looks nothing like Danny Glover and is dead. But his ghost
still walks the halls of our family home. We have moved
zip codes states regions weather zones and there is a thing
that is always with us.
I recognize the way she is poured
into her dress: the way we have poured slop into a trough
thinking it beneath us to touch the pigs' food, but somehow
not too good to feed off the slaughter. Of my grandmother's body,
I can say this: I have her slight breasts
and though they are not mine, I carried her slim hips
long enough to give them to my youngest.
What I had, what I did not keep, what I buried in the sandy soil of twenty
is her taste in men—the instinct
to pour myself into her hand-me-down muslin voice.
It's the back. That is what Whoopi Goldberg got perfect:
Miss Celie's back—
how it curves itself into the inflection of my grandmother's
every sentence. She hasn't declared anything in years.
Embeds a plea for permission in even hello.
I was wide-eyed finger-point when I saw us there
on the TV. What a luxury then, to watch that woman,
curse without inflection.

THINGS I WANT TO SAY TO RAE DAWN CHONG

Rae, I want to call you Rae.

———

Rae, you don't have hair like mine but—close enough, so I think I understand your dilemma, Rae. You should have been in more movies.

———

You always make me think of *The Jeffersons* even though you were never on that show. The neighbors were two-tone comic relief. Nothing like my parents. But you and Arnold in *Commando*. Oh, Rae, you two were unlikely and perfect and snapshot one-liner. You were the first people on TV that I understood. You had nothing in common. My father hated grits. My mother is from the south, Rae. Do you understand? What do the Chinese and Scottish or the Africans and the Canadians have in common except you?

———

You might think I would be crush-and-yearn watching *Soul Man* but C. Thomas Howell only got the skin right. Plus, you two were so perfect together: young and promising and pretending to be black. Rae, what did the casting calls say? Was it as straightforward as "brown?" As honest as "almost black?"

———

When you were cast in that movie, it was like you came home to me. Me and C. Thomas Howell. There's a scene, all soundtrack and moral, when the archetypal wizened black professor says to your blackened boyfriend: "You've learned something I can't teach them. You've learned what it feels like to be black." This is the moment on every VHS copy of that movie when I can hear white America sighing and commiserating and imagining checks made out to the NAACP and handed to a dignified black man in a tuxedo at a ceremony held in their honor. But then C. Thomas Howell says: "I don't really know what it feels like, sir. If I didn't like it, I could always get out." The quick sudden inhale of all those pale faces, the glow of the television casting them whiter than they are. The living room sucker-punch, quick as a line of dialogue.

———

But the professor offered a reprieve: "You've learned a great deal more than I thought."
What did you learn, Rae? All those years you spent as a black woman, your Chinese and Scottish and Irish and Canadian tucked into your pocket neat as a freedman's papers.

I SIT, FRAMED

He says that he obviously isn't racist
because of me
and I smile, nod, look away.
I know what you mean is not the same thing as
you're right
or even, *that makes sense.*
He jokes about bringing the picture to work:
Me, him, the kids on vacation
five inches tall, standing on his desk—
soft focus and stupid grin.
Then maybe, he says, maybe
the secretary who remembers
water fountains and the smell of burning
will, if not forgive him his skin,
at least, look past it
and see mine.

THE WOMEN IN THE FAMILY

Walking anywhere with my aunt makes a woman small;
no one compliments a shadow.
Every errand we ran, they stopped her:
The men, I did not understand why,
looked for a silent breath too long before the
stammering or the rehearsed lines or the impromptu sincerity.
The women wanted to pull it out of her,
whatever secret scent or shade or brand.
Her smile was so disarming
all at once *this is not for you* and *no* and
they never left angry.
The year my father died, men bloomed all over our yard
I tripped on them after school
trying to walk up the familiar masonry of our steps
they did not smell like jasmine even as they inched
toward our front door.
My mother, by then a blade without an appetite, offered them only
the reliable cut of her civility and it was never enough
to discourage them.
Four hundred pounds,
dressed in a floral print tarp and losing her hair,
my grandmother flirted with everyone
even when everyone was a 27-years-her-junior, gay, white, male doctor
who never made housecalls
except to her.
Every day when my grandfather came back home,
Man, you better call first
I barely had time to get my boyfriend out the back door.
A teasing threat, a joke

with its foot planted firmly on the ground.
My father's sisters made good German potato salad
and had a delightful assortment of decorative soaps.
I was a sad child: someone called me white once
and I half-believed them.

FAMILY MYTHOLOGY

In the made-for-TV movie, his jeans are blue
and so are her eyes
but no one notices just yet.
There is a black boy sweeping.
He doesn't have a name in the story.
If this were a documentary,
his name would be underneath his face
and underneath that would be his job title:
Shit Work.
He is 14 or 23 or 19. He is black.
It is 1955 or 1964 or 1971.
It does not matter how old he is. He is a—
Boy,
what are doing? Lazy good for nothing.
Didn't I tell you to sweep out the back room?
Then there are more words but she
never repeats them. The light has changed
and the voice belongs to the owner.
He enters stage left, long after his voice has
heralded his arrival. He surveys
all of the land: the meat slicer, the ovens, the counters
the greasers in the corner, the blond girl mute as
a bench on a bus,
the windows and the refrigerators.
He calls the boy something and then
the music changes.
There are several well-defined still shots:
The girl, her bluest eyes, her reddest cheeks.
The boy, his inhale and hold, his learned patience.

The baron of all, his contempt and accusation
funneled down to just one finger.
The music changes and the hero of the story, her hero,
the up-til-now ne'er-do-well in the corner
rising from his chair, from amidst his hoodlum compatriots
in slow motion.
In the myth, she is
a cashier. Her hands are swans,
they fly over the click and whistle
of the register. The deli serves thin slices
of Motown and thinner
slices of turkey
they melt
on his tongue and made him think
he was Smokey.
When she tells the kids the story,
he is a brute, an ogre
in a leather jacket. He is pomade
and cars that do not belong to him.
She puts the plate down on his table.
It is just pizza, nothing can be more
fairy-tale-perfect than pizza
in Jersey City. His bad grammar reaches out to her
Try to forget about me, darling, I'm no good for you.
His friends watch and listen.
He is not usually this honest but he is usually
this arrogant, this slick. She
is a police officer
and he is talking himself out of something

using dimples
and exaggerated hand gestures.
In the remake, there is a knife fight.
There is a large aquarium. In one of the endings,
the hoodlum-turned-hero drowns the man
and the water conveniently drenches our fair maid,
her all-American breasts are cold and perfect and perky.
In the graphic novel, there is an entire frame
dedicated to the girl's face
as she watches the boy who knows his smile is charming
stand up and yell at the owner of the pizzeria
in Jersey City. He is defending the honor of some
nice black boy that he never met before.
She is imagining her own honor
kept warm by the leather jacket
he'll throw over her shoulders after their first date
so *No, Darling*, she won't forget about him
and if he is no good
he is at least a good story
and your children,
and heartwarming major movie house releases
need heroes:
Nice white boys saving us all and still
underneath the black boy's face it says everything important about him:
Black.

Casual Racist

I'm having dinner with the casual racist which is to say that I'm having
dinner with a friend and a friend of that friend which is to say: there is
no safe place.

I am having dinner with the casual racist when he says, after a thought-
ful head tilt—which is clearly meant to indicate that he has considered,
at length, what he is about to say *he*, the casual racist points to my son,
looks like your husband but your girls, he chin nods in the direction of the
double helix hurricane of elbows, laughter, and errant silverware, *your
girls take after you.*

This is to say that the casual racist noticed over dinner
only what a stranger might notice in the street
and nothing more.

To be fair, my youngest daughter looks like a photo of me at age 3: In it,
I am doubled over with laughter. But my oldest daughter is her father's
girl, has his Sunday morning smile, his never-idle hands, his everything.
All of this is to say that the casual racist has noticed our skin, but not our
faces: we are all brown, my girls and me, so we must look like each other.
My son is proof of everything I learned in 8th grade science class
about Punnett's square and chance. To be honest, I never thought
I would see my father's blue eyes again, let alone staring up at me
from my child's face, which is to say I imagine the casual racist as a child,
a kindergartener, oh! how he must have excelled at sorting,
at putting like with like
which is to say—no which is to ask: How can we possibly be a family?
Which is to say: this is too complicated and it scares him.
Which is to say: there is a long American history of people who look
like us—all our many faces.
Which is to say my family is not groundbreaking. Not new, not novel,
not even surprising,

which to say: invisible.
I am eating dinner with the casual racist, a friend of a friend, who is
talking to me about my children and he hasn't seen any of us
which is to say: there is no safe place.

THRESHOLD

I don't want to go in
but it's my house
and eventually I will run out of benches
out of sidewalks
out of other houses that I never belonged in.
I will have to go home.
When I do
I walk over each wide-planked body
in the entryway.
They creak under my weight
but do not give.
I try not to see them
as I step
my heel bruising their foreheads, cheeks, thighs
as I walk to the kitchen.
I don't remember when they were installed,
I think I inherited them with the house
But maybe never noticed until
one day
I opened the door
and there, under each foot, a face:
The woman from the coffee shop who touched my hair
as if it were a sweater she might buy
but only if it were soft enough
and did not talk back.
The boy who thought he was complimenting me
by imagining some distance between my mother's face and mine.
The cashier who asked more than once
whose children I was babysitting

and recoiled every time they said, *mama*.
This is who nips at my toes.
This is what I am walking through
and, when I come home, what I am trying to escape.

The Children Speak:

1.
I have four years old.
I have a ring my mimi gave me at the store when I'm a grownup I'll
give it to my husband and we'll dance like the friends in the pictures on
the hallway wall mama says I don't have to get married or have babies
she says babies is hard and a lot of work she smiles and hugs me when
she says it and at night after the story she hugs us all a family hug there
are one two three four five of us but she has big arms

2.
I am four.
When I am five I can get my ears pieced like mama she says it will hurt
but only for a minute like a shot at the doctors office she says we already
have earrings but no holes to put them in she has holes in her ears and
in her nose but not us my sister is afraid she said no mama said it's your
body and finished fixing her hair I said yes mama said it's your body
and then it was my turn to get my hair fixed I like it out my face not
like mama she only looks nice when it's out her face but she don't never
wear it like that

3.
I'm am three.
I like gramma and mimi my sister only likes mimi my sister likes gram-
ma and mimi but mimi more i like my moms mom she say put that
arm up and tickle me she don't look like me but look like mama and i
love mama she got mama's face her notsmile her madvoice gramma a
lot like mama i like gramma

1.

I ask everyday when she's gonna finish working she always say in a few minutes I ask why she work so much she ask if I like eating I do I like corn toasters I say this morning that her and daddy need to buy more when they go to the store she say that's why she working

2.

Mama doesn't play outside with us like Daddy does she watches us through the screendoor and fixes us water in our water bottles we come in and she says don't run in the house Daddy is outside on the trampoline showing us how to do flips mama's feet never leave the ground

3.

We been outside for forever my neck hurts it's pink like Daddy's my sisters their necks don't hurt they never hurt or turn pink Imma go inside and get water and sun lotion from mama and come back Daddy is teaching me how to jump big

1.

I have a twin but I look like my mama not just like my mama like my mama don't look just like gramma she's brown dark brown mama is light brown I don't have a color for me i wish I was pink and purple striped daddy don't have a color either but not like me like baby boy he only a color when he pink i wish I was pink and purple striped

2.

Mama never cuts our hair 'cept baby boy she says we black I don't know what that means I'm brown like her and gramma gramma say white and black in whispers but I hear her mimi never say black or white and she turn the TV when one of the people on there say it mimi wears her hair short out of her face she ask mama when she gonna cut our hair mama say we're black and mimi turn pink

3.
I like green the best I want to be a turtle sometimes I like suncolor yellow is sometimes my favorite I tell mama my favorite and she get her sadface I ask why she don't like yellow she don't answer til her unhappymouth say I love you

WHEN I HAD CHILDREN WITH A WHITE PERSON

I spent nine months rubbing cocoa butter
on all that swollen worry
remembered the name of my dead baby uncle
Googled too many times "congenital
heart abnormality" and blood
I avoided it afraid it would come unwanted
and sudden in my lap
I did not think I should re-watch *Roots*
my partner did not watch *Birth of a Nation* there was no
Imitation of Life date night when the fear slid
a bone thin finger up my thigh
my partner's hand, despite its paleness
held me and saw me through it
I did not wish for someone else
even someone else more like me
a woman unprovoked
said to us in a store *how beautiful your kids will be*
I wanted to show her my teeth
what of an animal
do you examine to judge its health
what tells the scientists if a thing is meant to bite
no one called our children niggers that day but
there are a lot of ways to say
my child born under a knife   our family visits
all the school administrators asks for other faces
like mine   say diversity   say white supremacy   say we
expect better   we   both of us   expect
to celebrate Christmas I had to take it
when it was offered me not a tradition, I held or

wanted my partner's pale hand rubs cocoa butter
on the children because my grandmother lotioned me
we are a smooth-kneed family
I say *if you don't get your narrow black ass over here*
to a child light as my partner
but black as me my mother said it first
she did not need to say no baby
we don't make pumpkin pie   in our house
we say family in both of our mouths with every tongue we have

//IF YOU SAY IT IS.

my mother knows Jesus//better than I know//anyone//can say, "I am//a saviour."//anyone// can promise//forgiveness//is free// when the sin wasn't against you// watch: I absolve//your mother her ill-timed laugh//her too-long silence//and then//her too quick-tongue//look//it's gone//the oldest magic// the disappearance//a grievance subsumed//by a prayer//in your name// I say these words//here//is my name//say it in remembrance of me//that you might know me//half as well//as I want to know him//I want to know him//the way mother//says his name// I think I know Jesus//too//many times//I read his book//I know how it ends//for me//I don't begrudge//the ghost//writers translating that man//into someone// my mother//could love//invite the revisionist to my deathbed//when you say my name//tell me better//than I am//at my funeral//say I did magic once//say she knew me//say I knew her//better than anyone//and make me, then//into a useful thing:// a god//requires only time//and a mouth// with enough hollow teeth//to store everyone's grief//and a mouth//to say that one//is mine//the clay-footed//the pierced//the flawed and fleshed//I know// that one//like my own children// I want to have my own//Jesus// my own//god//his mouth open and waiting//for me//this is what I got instead:// her//mouth spinning a thick and deep rope//of grief//Judas hung himself//because he couldn't believe//what he'd done//for love//of money// and of history//but I know his name//too//many times we tell the story//as if we'd remember it//absent its villain//so say// my mother's god//is a sweet song//and I can learn anything//if I hear it enough times//when I go//say I did a magic trick once//say I knew you//say absolved//say forgave//say believed//until you know my name//by heart//I promise you//it's all true

I Wish I Was More Mothers

After Brenda Shaunessey

One to take the picture, another to be in it
One more still to apply the filter and type #nofilter
One to pin the things on Pinterest
One to collect the pine cones and organize the glitter
and buy the 12 X 12 crafting paper and vellum
One to schedule the photo shoot and to slick each child's hair
to buy the matching outfits and iron each one
to stiff perfection
One to say fuck it and let the hoard of them go
to school in whatever they want
One to send out the holiday cards
to handwrite the addresses
to buy the personalized stamps and send them
well before the season passes
One to match each small sock to its lonely mate
and not only wash, but fold and even put away, the laundry
One to pay the wash and fold service
One to just buy new clothes
One to learn to sew, to mend, to darn everything
we break with our bodies
One to make dinner
to try the new recipes from a curated list of mommy blogs
One to mommy blog: to package each day
into less
than one thousand words and a moral
the other moms might be shamed
into pretending to believe
One to be condescending
One to be shamed

One to breastfeed in public: areola casually displayed
as we, the clucking and laughing mothers, eat guacamole at a local
organic eatery
One to breastfeed
in the bathroom with the wafting aroma
of urine to remind me of my place
One to breastfeed at home between the private walls
and jags of crying
One to cry non-stop for years
in private and, in public, to look, unblinking,
at the other mothers' ironed pants
and perfect eye makeup
One to lament the life we will never live
One to brunch
One to develop an unhealthy reliance on alcohol
or brownies or pills or another woman
whose sadness and understanding makes her me
One to have the affair
One to repent
Another to schedule the marriage
counseling, to write the appointments on the large dry erase calendar
One to bump into it in the night and wipe it blank with an errant shoulder
One to walk the dogs, feed the fish, change the litterbox
One to say no: the house is too small
for one more living thing
One to fall out of love and leave
One to fall out of love and stay
One to stay in love
and leave anyway

One to listen to all the saddest songs
and stay
listening
One to fuck like childless women do: with abandon and the blade
of consequence inches above the impending orgasm
One to fuck like a mother: as if the worst
has already happened, as if the best
has already happened, as if today,
now, the orgasm makes the laundry doable
One to fuck like a mother who has forgotten her children:
moaning too loud
mouth too open
walls too thin
thinking they'll have to learn somehow
One to make the lunches
One to tell the nanny to make the lunches
One to say find your own fucking lunch for once
One to stay home
to sweep
to clean
to know where each toy is likely hiding
to think: what am I giving up to be here?
One to go out into the market: to earn
to wonder
where the children are in this exact moment
as the projector fails or the manager scolds or the shirt's seams face outward
like a neon sign announcing who we really are.
to think: what am I giving up
to be here

One to kiss the babies
to miracle small scrapes into laughter
One to laugh
One to say to the rest of us: *we are doing okay*
we are doing what needs to be done
One to call our mothers and forgive
or accuse. One to answer when the call comes for us

ACKNOWLEDGEMENTS

Many thanks to the editors of the following publications in which these poems first appeared, sometimes in earlier versions: *Muzzle Magazine* ("Things Only a Black Mother Can Prepare You For"); *The Offing* ("Motherhood" and "But If You are a White Boy, Then My Father was a White Boy, Too."); *Yellow Chair Review* ("The Woman Who Is Not the Nanny Answers at the Grocery Store Concerning the, Evidently, Mismatched Children In and Around Her Cart"); *Drunk in a Midnight Choir* ("The Paper Trail" and "I Have Counted Sixteen and a Half Deer on My Ride Home From Work"); *FreezeRay* ("Things I Want to Say to Rae Dawn Chong"); and *The Collagist* ("Conception" and "Townies").

———

My gratitude to the women in my life: my mother who is a machete and a balm, my aunt Beryl who shaped my definition of beautiful, my gramma Sue, my gramma Tina, my Allison, Haley, my sisters Nadia and Candace, the ladies of BNP who stay dreaming and working, and Sydney and Fiona who teach me.

My thanks to the men in my life: my father who taught me how to build and grieve things, my brothers Marc and Josh whose talents inspire me, my Grandpop who loved cards and bad jokes, my Thomas who made me kick my mother just by speaking to me, Will and Omar who reminded how seriously I take my fun, Philo who teaches me, and Chad. Always Chad.

ABOUT THE AUTHOR

Nicole Homer's writing has appeared in *Muzzle, The Offing, Freez-eRay Poetry, Cease Cows, The Boiler Journal,* and elsewhere. She is an Editor and regular contributor at BlackNerdProblems. She has an MFA from Rutgers–Newark and currently lives in New Jersey where she teaches. She lives online at www.nicolehomer.com

If You Like Nicole Homer,
Nicole Likes...

Racing Hummingbirds — Jeanann Verlee
Said the Manic to the Muse — Jeanann Verlee
I Love Science! — Shanny Jean Maney
Aim for the Head: An Anthology of Zombie Poetry — Rob Sturma, Editor

Write Bloody Publishing distributes and promotes great books of poetry every year. We are an independent press dedicated to quality literature and book design.

Our employees are authors and artists so we call ourselves a family. Our design team comes from all over America: modern painters, photographers and rock album designers create book covers we're proud to be judged by.

We have published over 115 titles to date. We are grass-roots, D.I.Y., bootstrap believers. Pull up a good book and join the family. Support independent authors, artists and presses.

Want to know more about Write Bloody books, authors and events?
Join our mailing list at

www.writebloody.com

WRITE BLOODY BOOKS

After the Witch Hunt — Megan Falley

Aim for the Head: An Anthology of Zombie Poetry — Rob Sturma, Editor

Amulet — Jason Bayani

Any Psalm You Want — Khary Jackson

Birthday Girl with Possum — Brendan Constantine

The Bones Below — Sierra DeMulder

Born in the Year of the Butterfly Knife — Derrick C. Brown

Bring Down the Chandeliers — Tara Hardy

Ceremony for the Choking Ghost — Karen Finneyfrock

Courage: Daring Poems for Gutsy Girls — Karen Finneyfrock,
    Mindy Nettifee & Rachel McKibbens, Editors

Dear Future Boyfriend — Cristin O'Keefe Aptowicz

Dive: The Life and Fight of Reba Tutt — Hannah Safren

Drunks and Other Poems of Recovery — Jack McCarthy

The Elephant Engine High Dive Revival anthology

Everything Is Everything — Cristin O'Keefe Aptowicz

The Feather Room — Anis Mojgani

Gentleman Practice — Buddy Wakefield

Glitter in the Blood: A Guide to Braver Writing — Mindy Nettifee

Good Grief — Stevie Edwards

The Good Things About America — Derrick Brown & Kevin Staniec, Editors

Hot Teen Slut — Cristin O'Keefe Aptowicz

I Love Science! — Shanny Jean Maney

I Love You Is Back — Derrick C. Brown

The Importance of Being Ernest — Ernest Cline

In Search of Midnight — Mike McGee

The Incredible Sestina Anthology — Daniel Nester, Editor

Junkyard Ghost Revival anthology

Kissing Oscar Wilde — Jade Sylvan

The Last Time as We Are — Taylor Mali

Learn Then Burn — Tim Stafford & Derrick C. Brown, Editors

Learn Then Burn Teacher's Manual — Tim Stafford &
    Molly Meacham, Editors

Live for a Living — Buddy Wakefield

Love in a Time of Robot Apocalypse — David Perez

The Madness Vase — Andrea Gibson

My, My, My, My, My — Tara Hardy

The New Clean — Jon Sands

New Shoes on a Dead Horse — Sierra DeMulder

No Matter the Wreckage — Sarah Kay

Oh God Get Out Get Out — Bill Moran

Oh, Terrible Youth — Cristin O'Keefe Aptowicz

Ordinary Cruelty — Amber Flame

The Oregon Trail Is the Oregon Trail — Gregory Sherl

Over the Anvil We Stretch — Anis Mojgani

Pecking Order — Nicole Homer

The Pocket Knife Bible — Anis Mojgani

Pole Dancing to Gospel Hymns — Andrea Gibson

Racing Hummingbirds — Jeanann Verlee

Redhead and the Slaughter King — Megan Falley

Rise of the Trust Fall — Mindy Nettifee

Said the Manic to the Muse — Jeanann Verlee

Scandalabra — Derrick C. Brown

Slow Dance with Sasquatch — Jeremy Radin

The Smell of Good Mud — Lauren Zuniga

Songs from Under the River — Anis Mojgani

Spiking the Sucker Punch — Robbie Q. Telfer

Strange Light — Derrick C. Brown

Stunt Water — Buddy Wakefield

These Are the Breaks — Idris Goodwin

Time Bomb Snooze Alarm — Bucky Sinister

The Undisputed Greatest Writer of All Time — Beau Sia

Uh-Oh — Derrick Brown

What Learning Leaves — Taylor Mali

What the Night Demands — Miles Walser

Working Class Represent — Cristin O'Keefe Aptowicz

Write About an Empty Birdcage — Elaina Ellis

Yarmulkes & Fitted Caps — Aaron Levy Samuels

The Year of No Mistakes — Cristin O'Keefe Aptowicz

Yesterday Won't Goodbye — Brian S. Ellis